ADAM LEARNS TEAMWORK

Dalia Ramzi Mohammad

Editor: Noor Hammoud
Copyright ©2019 by Dalia Ramzi Mohammad

"Go Adam!" the crowd cheered.
Adam dribbled the basketball down the court.
He aimed for the net and shot.
Swoosh! He scored!
The crowd jumped for joy.

It was now the other team's turn.
Adam rushed in and stole the ball.
As he sprinted down the court,
his teammates called his name.
They wanted him to pass to them,
but Adam refused.
He shot again and scored.
The crowd cheered,
but his teammates did not.

Later in the game,

Adam got the ball again.

His teammates pleaded,

"Adam, please pass us the ball!"

Adam ignored them and did not share.

Then he jumped up to shoot but got blocked.

The other team grabbed the ball.

They shot, scored, and won the game.

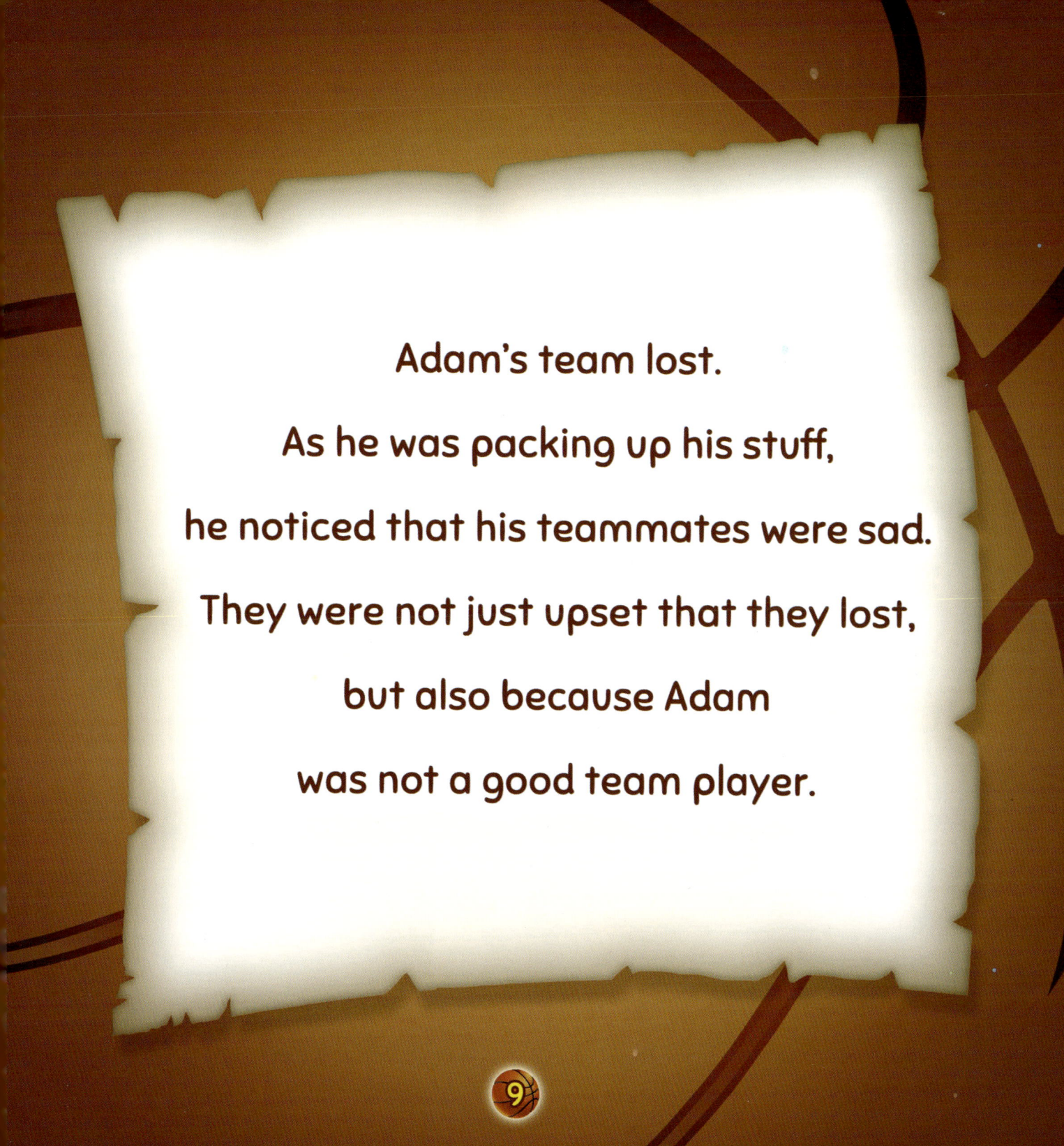

Adam's team lost.

As he was packing up his stuff,

he noticed that his teammates were sad.

They were not just upset that they lost,

but also because Adam

was not a good team player.

As Adam walked home,

he thought about his sad teammates.

He realized that he did not share at all.

He felt bad.

Then he remembered how Allah

loves for us to be humble,

not show off,

and to work together.

Before the next game,
Adam called his teammates over.
"I'm sorry I did not pass the ball,"
he said.
"From now on, I'm going to share."
This time when he got the ball
he passed it to his teammate,
who then scored! They won the game!

When the game was finished,

the crowd cheered.

Adam was happy

and so were his teammates.

It was a great game!

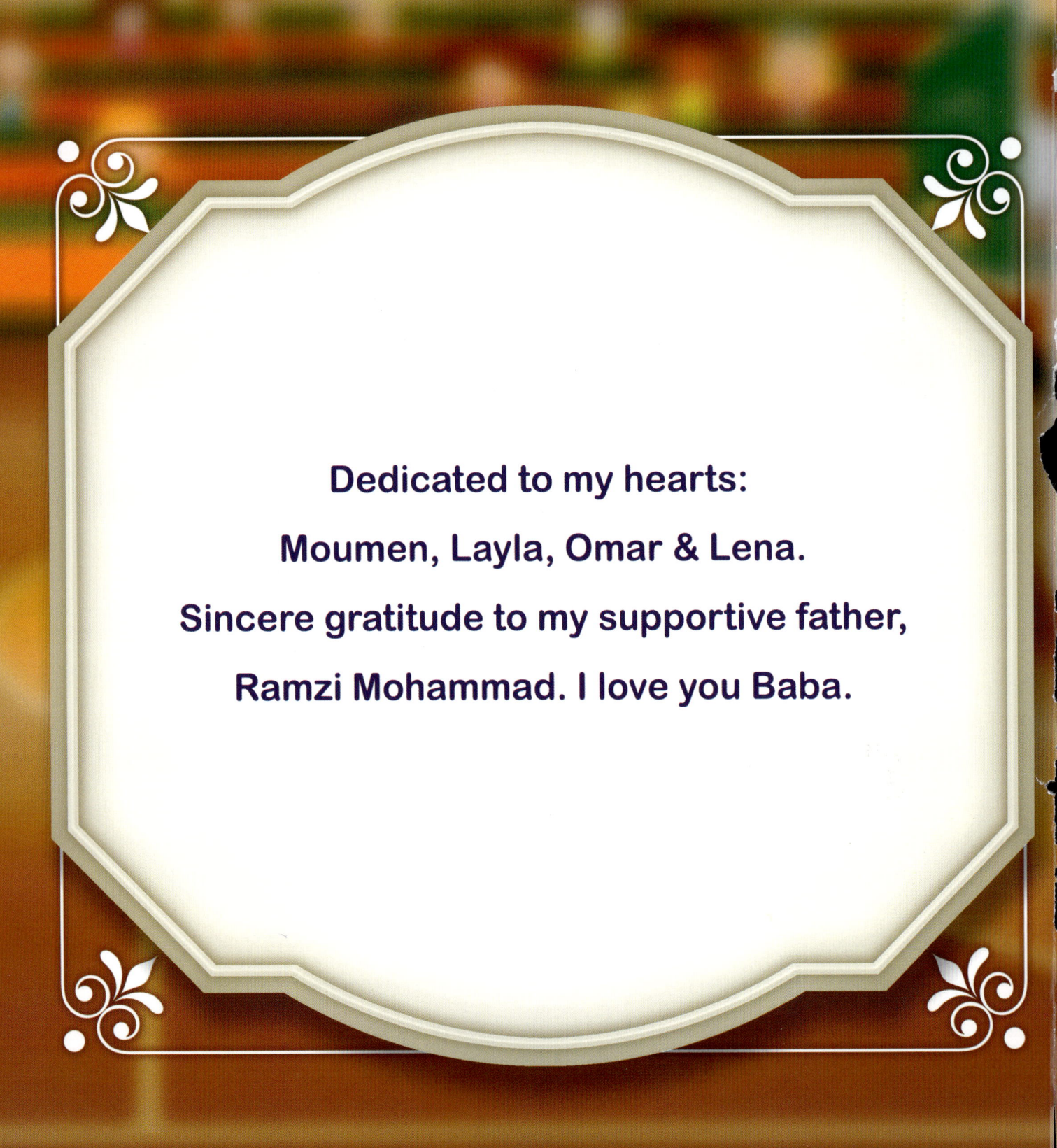

Dedicated to my hearts:

Moumen, Layla, Omar & Lena.

Sincere gratitude to my supportive father,

Ramzi Mohammad. I love you Baba.

Sara and Adam series

ADAM LEARNS TEAMWORK

Dalia Ramzi Mohammad